PAST AND FUTURE ISSUE

We'll go where no one has gone before!
And... to places where others have
definitely already gone before. Then,
after all that racing around, we'll try
to be HERE, right now.

11 12 1
10 2
9 3
8 4
7 6 5

FROM US TO YOU...

RESULTS

OTHER:
(fill in the blank)
15.4%

SPACESHIP
23.1%

HOVERCRAFT
7.7%

BULLET TRAIN
15.4%

ZEPPELIN
7.7%

CANOE
30.8%

contributors:

Charlotte Ager, Zubair Ahmed, Alex Aldrich Barrett, Jessixa Bagley,
Aaron Bagley, Julie Benbassat, Tom Bingham, Aaron Gonzalez, David Huang,
Katharina Kulenkampff, Muzzy, Andy Chou Musser, Alejandra Oviedo,
Ysidro Pergamino, Weng Pixin, Jim Pluk, and Valerio Vidali

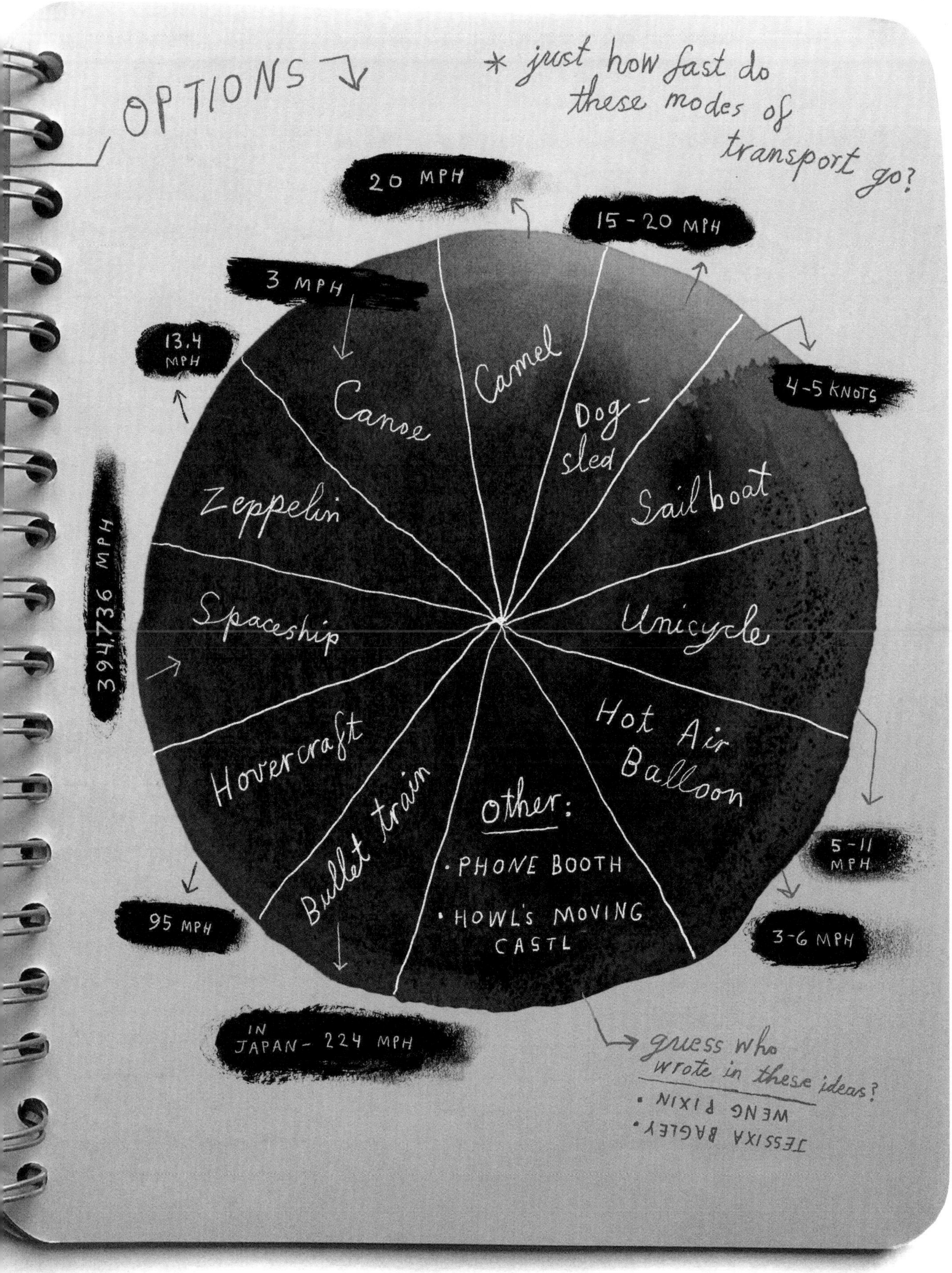

OPTIONS ↓

* just how fast do these modes of transport go?

20 MPH

15 - 20 MPH

3 MPH

13.4 MPH

4 - 5 KNOTS

394.736 MPH

Canoe

Camel

Dog-sled

Sailboat

Zeppelin

Spaceship

Unicycle

Hovercraft

Hot Air Balloon

Bullet train

Other:
• PHONE BOOTH
• HOWL'S MOVING CASTL

5 - 11 MPH

3 - 6 MPH

95 MPH

IN JAPAN - 224 MPH

→ guess who wrote in these ideas?

• JESSIXA BAGLEY
• WENG PIXIN

inside

iLLUSTORIA

MEET SPECIAL GUESTS

cover artist
CHARLOTTE AGER

guest writers
JESSIXA & AARON BAGLEY

guest poet
ZUBAIR AHMED

chapter comics
JIM PLUK

typographic artist
YSIDRO PERGAMINO

CHAPTER 1

LAUGH AND PLAY

GRAB A FRIEND & TRY THESE!

CHAPTER 2

READ AND LEARN

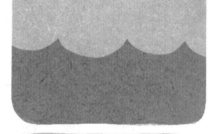

ILLUSTORIA IS THE
OFFICIAL PUBLICATION
OF THE INTERNATIONAL
ALLIANCE OF YOUTH
WRITING CENTERS

OUR CHAPTER PAGES IN THIS ISSUE FEATURE TYPOGRAPHICAL ART BY YSIDRO PERGAMINO

LAUGH AND PLAY

SAY WHAT!?

MATCH THE SAYING TO THE IMAGE   art by AARON GONZALEZ

No, no, no I meant PEAS on Earth, not PEACE on Earth!

Professor Robot at your service.

My hair always does this when I'm nervous...

Will you accept this intergalactic call?

See you on the dark side of the moon, dear friend.

Are you thinking what I'm thinking?

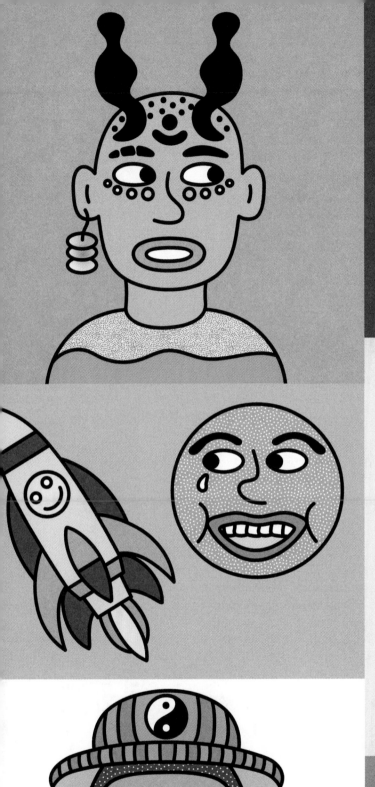

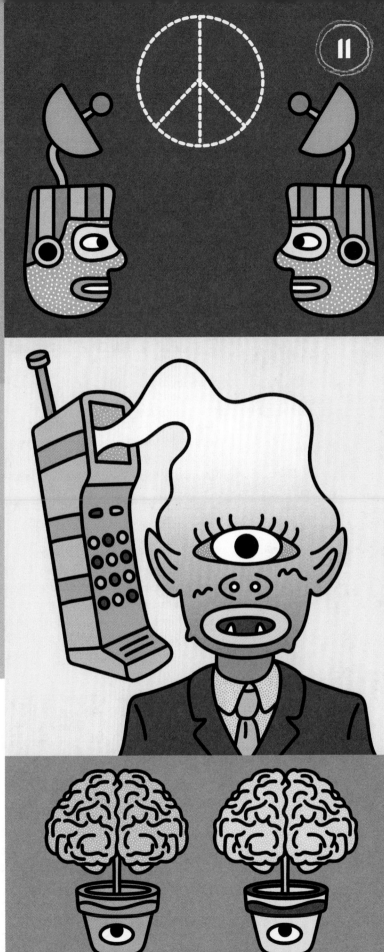

Story Starters > TIME-TRAVEL-DINING!
Words by Amy Sumerton

For this issue's Story Starters, we're going to *dip* into different eras... Do you have an *appetite* for imaginative thinking?

Writers often, metaphorically, *chew* on their own curiosities and make *meals* out of the results. Sure, we're *plating* up a lot of puns, but next, we're going to practice this in a very literal way!

Living creatures—past, present, and (we can pretty safely assume!) future—need certain things to live. One of the most important (and delicious!) categories of basic needs for human beings is (have you already guessed where this is going)... food!

People have been making and serving and eating food basically since the dawn of time. And all signs point to them continuing to do so... forever.

So, consider yourself cordially invited to dinner! Actually, to four different dinners. In four different time periods! Our character is Rose, a famed time-traveler and restaurateur. Rose is putting together diners in some of her favorite eras.

NOW, YOU VISIT EACH OF THESE DINERS AND DESCRIBE YOUR EXPERIENCE!

What does the atmosphere look like?

Write a story as someone visiting each diner for a meal.

Write reviews of each diner from the point of view of a time-traveling food critic.

Write day-in-the-life stories as employees who work at each diner (server, chef, dishwasher).

How does the food taste? smell?

What are the other visitors wearing and talking about?

260 BCE

ROSE'S DINER

ROASTED BONE
MARROW

–

BROTH OF WILD
MUSHROOMS

–

ACORN BREAD
AND
GOOSEBERRIES

1886 CE

Rose's Diner

Turtle Punch
Truffle-scented Egg Salad
Pigeons à la Crème or Leg of Duck
Tangerine Sorbet with Frosted Grapes

ROSE'S DI-NER

Sesame Shrimp
Fingers (4)   – appetizer

Veggie Yakisoba Taco – mild

Kimchi Quesadilla – spicy!

Tofu Green Tea   – add a
Layer Cake   scoop of
                              Lychee ice
                              cream
                              & xtra

2024

ROSE'S
DINER - LABORATORY

1.   2.   3.

NUTRIENT
SHAPES

ARCTIC
FRUIT
STACK

* [EXPERIMENTAL]
SEA SALT
SLUSHIE

* WARNING

2999

THE NIGHT RIDERS

Matt Furie

In Matt Furie's glorious debut, a nocturnal frog and rat awake at midnight, share a salad of lettuce and bugs, and strike out on an epic dirtbike adventure toward the sunrise. Find *The Night Riders*, and many other books, at the link below.

THE NIGHT RIDERS

Matt Furie

ANCIENT ARCTIC WORMS DEFROSTED!

Did you know that a recently discovered ancient species of worm, found in a defrosted iceberg that is at least 46,000 years old, came back to life when it was thawed?

Test your survival skills inside this maze of icebergs and slithering worms!

by KATHARINA KULENKAMPFF

Laugh and play

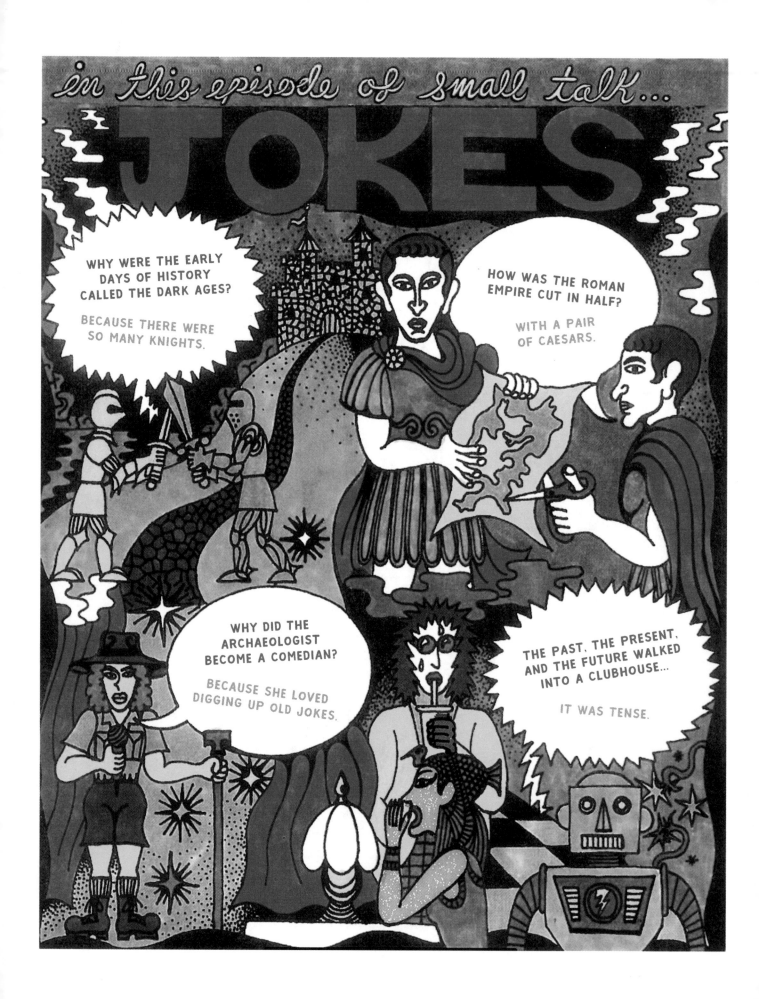

Fascinating FACTOIDS

THE HISTORY OF THE STARRY SKY ART BY MUZZY

ANCIENT POLYNESIANS LEARNED TO USE THE STARS TO NAVIGATE THOUSANDS OF MILES ACROSS THE PACIFIC OCEAN.

ANCIENT EGYPTIANS TRACKED THE RISING TIME OF THE BRIGHT STAR SIRIUS, WHOSE YEARLY CYCLE ALWAYS PRECEDED THE FLOODING OF THE RIVER NILE, WHICH THEY USED FOR IRRIGATING CROPS.

THE MAYANS CREATED THE 11TH- OR 12TH-CENTURY DRESDEN CODEX. MEASURING TWELVE FEET LONG, ITS ACCORDION-FOLD PAGES CONTAIN HIEROGLYPHS DEPICTING ASTRONOMICAL TABLES BASED ON THOUSANDS OF YEARS OF OBSERVATION.

ARISTARCHUS OF SAMOS (310 B.C.E.-230 B.C.E) WAS RESPONSIBLE FOR THE EARLIEST-KNOWN THEORY OF THE SOLAR SYSTEM WHICH PLACED THE SUN AT THE CENTER WITH ALL THE PLANETS ROTATING AROUND IT. THIS MODEL OF THE UNIVERSE WAS NOT WIDELY ACCEPTED UNTIL 1,400 YEARS LATER.

TYPOGRAPHICAL ART BY YSIDRO PERGAMINO

YOU ARE HERE

A JOURNEY INTO THE TIME SPACE CONTINUUM

by Jessixa & Aaron Bagley, art by Andy Chou Musser

PAST

So, people are always talking about the past and the future and how to travel into those realms. But the truth of the matter is... get this... there is no such place as the past or the future! Mind-bending, right? There is only right-now-the-present—this very second—which truly exists. Let's talk about how that affects the past first.

Wait, if the past doesn't exist, then why are people always talking about it?

Because that's where we keep experiences, feelings, memories of awkward family gatherings, and bad haircuts.

Oh, I actually have a picture to verify that last one.

Boo!

The past is an idea. A reflection of a present moment that is long gone. You can't avoid the current moment because it's **always** happening. Hot dogs. See? You couldn't escape randomly reading "hot dogs" just then, and now you can't take it back. It's too late. It lives in your memories and will haunt your dreams.

You ARE Here

Even if you had a machine that would allow you to choose to insert yourself ANYwhere in the Space-Time Continuum... when you got there, you'd still be in the present moment... in THAT time period. You're always in YOUR own present moment, even if you took that into the past. Right?

I'm not sure. What about the idea if you go back in time there will be duplicates of yourself?

We don't have time to talk about that.

Well then how does time travel work in the Future?

Let's go see...

Oooo! A portal!

POSSIBLE WAYS TO STOP TIME

REMOTE CONTROL

TOUCHING YOUR TWO FINGERS TOGETHER

MAKING A "T" FOR "TIME OUT" WITH YOUR HANDS

FUTURE

Okay, so we told you that only the present exists and there is no past. But we also said there is no future. We aren't trying to bum you out... promise. We just mean that the future is an idea too. The future is where a lot of great ideas live! Like hope, possibilities, and the promise of cake at your friend's birthday party. But since it's just an idea about what might happen, unless it's right in front of you, you can't eat a "cake promise."

> Don't touch the cake. We have to sing first.

> Booo. I never get Invisible Future Cake!

But just as you can't get to the past—the future is also impossible to get to. Remember the pausing-time thing? In order to get to the future, a similar miracle would have to happen—but this time everyone would need to be paused around you and YOU would need to be the one that keeps moving and growing. Then, when you un-paused time, everyone would have to catch up with you. While it lasts, it will be like you're in their future!

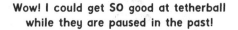

Honestly though, time travel can't exist because everyone is experiencing their own reality. Our son Baxter told us that if two people are looking at a rainbow, they are both seeing two different rainbows because they are looking at it from different angles.

We like that. It means that everything depends upon how you look at it. Maybe time is like that too. There might not be a past or a future, but there's a right now. And depending on how you look at the right now, it can look pretty good.

WE ASKED A POET...

ZUBAIR AHMED IS A POET-ENGINEER LIVING IN PORTLAND, OREGON. WE ASKED HIM TO READ AN ASTROPHYSICS ARTICLE TITLED, "IS TIME TRAVEL POSSIBLE?" HERE ARE HIS THOUGHTS.

art by ALEJANDRA OVIEDO

Did you know that time, gravity, and speed are all related?

Crank up gravity, crank up speed, say farewell to all the supportive people in your life, and

WHOOoo00SH ~~

deep into the future you go!

Wait, when you put it like that...

Why would anyone want to race into the future?

(silence)

(thinking)

What about traveling into the past?

Scientists agree, theoretically, that one can indeed travel into the past.

This means that according to complicated numbers and equations, there might be a very small chance.

So why hasn't it happened yet?

Oh, because these theories need stuff like negative mass and sasquatch hair – stuff that's still in the realm of the imagination.

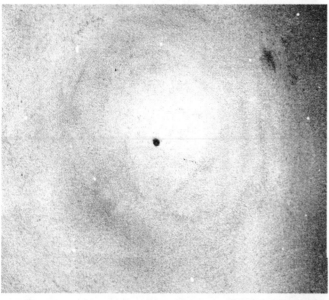

What does that say about our personal and collective pasts?

We're super sure that things have happened; otherwise how did things get to be the way they are?

Could it be that our memories and imaginations are the true time machines...

...and we're time-traveling every day?

The End.

CREATURE FEATURE

words *by* Amy Sumerton *art by* Julie Benbassat

Greetings, humans! Doc Anthurium—scientist and, ahem, an *actual flower*—here with you again today to learn more about some mysterious and inventive animal preservation strategies!

When you think of fossils, do you think of dinosaur bones? Permineralization is one of the most common processes by which fossils are formed. It occurs when minerals enter the pores of a dead organism. The minerals, over time, attach themselves to cell walls, and build a crystalline network. This process continues inside the walls until the main cavity of the cell, the lumen, is totally full. The cell walls themselves remain intact and surround the crystals.

An especially special thing about this process? This mineralization hardens the bone of, say, a dead dinosaur and essentially turns it into stone, preserving its original structure in a new form.

One way fossils are created is when an organism—an insect, arachnid, or small lizard—is trapped in amber. The process begins when the creature is covered in tree sap. Over time, the sap hardens, with the organism suspended within it, like a tomb. Thus, an insect preserved in amber is left unchanged. Scientists have been able to extract DNA from these fossils, giving us tons of important information about the past!

Not so for carbonization! This process changes an organism's soft tissue into thin, black films of carbon (a chemical element). This can happen when organisms are squeezed between layers of sediment. Compression occurs, and while larger organisms (like mammals) would be distorted, (uh, squished), perfect fossils of leaves and insects can result. An especially special thing about this? Many layers of carbonized plant material creates the fossil fuel: coal.

Another interesting way fossils have been created is in tar! Have you ever heard of the La Brea Tar Pits? Located in Los Angeles, California, the fossils unearthed here have delivered secrets from 40,000 to 8,000 years ago, and include plants, mollusks, and insects... as well as mammoths, sabre-toothed cats, longhorn bison, camels, and birds—over 660 species of organisms.

COMET VIEWING SCHEDULE

-an astronomical way to track Time

THE GREAT COMET OF 1744

WHICH ONES HAVE ALREADY PASSED?
WHEN IS THE NEXT ONE COMING?

words by Amy Sumerton

COMETS OF THE PAST

Arguably the most famous ball of ice and debris to cross our solar system ever is Halley's Comet. Halley's is special in part because it's easily visible to the naked eye from Earth every 75-79 years—so a person might be able to see it twice in their life!

(True fact, the person writing this saw it in 1986 as a fourth grader, and hopes to see the comet again in 2061, when she'll be 85.)

Other famous comets from history include:

* COMET DE CHÉSEAUX of 1744, seen with six tails
* DONATI'S COMET of 1858, first to be photographed
* THE GREAT COMET of 1861, discovered by a sheep farmer

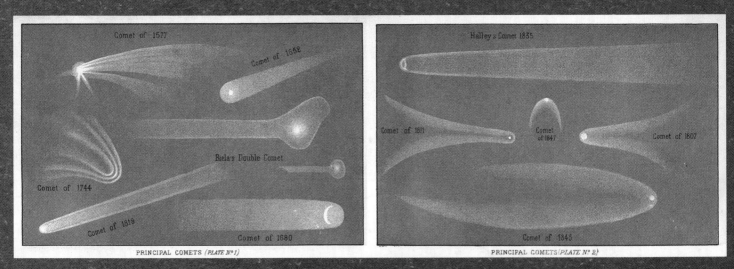

PRINCIPAL COMETS (PLATE Nº 1)

PRINCIPAL COMETS (PLATE Nº 2)

ALL COMETS COME FROM ONE OF TWO STRETCHES OF ICY DEBRIS LEFT OVER FROM THE FORMATION OF OUR SOLAR SYSTEM. ONE OF THE LARGEST OF THESE IS CALLED THE KUIPER BELT.

THE KUIPER BELT IS A BAGEL-SHAPED CLOUD OF ICY PARTICLES THAT FLOATS ABOUT THREE BILLION MILES FROM THE SUN (LIKE, BEYOND NEPTUNE!).

COMETS OF THE FUTURE

There are two kinds of comets: short form (whose elliptical journey around the sun takes under 200 years, like Halley's) and long form (whose journeys can take thousands of years to orbit the Sun).

Upcoming comets you might spot:

* COMET C/2023 A3, makes its approach on September 28, 2024, (although it might burn up and disappear before then!)

* HALLEY'S COMET - returns 2061

Wait—what <u>are</u> comets? Giant, dirty snowballs in SPACE?

Are they rocks? Are they ice? Are they dirt and dust? Are they time travelers?
(A: ALL OF THE ABOVE!)
A comet's nucleus—made up of ice, rock and other stuff like frozen gasses and dust—
ranges from less than a mile to a few dozen miles (!!!) in diameter.

Most of a comet's journey is cold and lonely, with the comet as a tail-less, very dark object
that is coated in layers of dust and other grimy particles; making it almost like a huge
chunk of charcoal. But, as the comet gets closer to the Sun (and starts to heat up), its ice
melts and pieces of dirt form a dusty cloud around the nucleus. Solar winds create separate
tails of dust and gas, aka the "long hairs" the ancient Greeks named them for!

* Flip to Deeper Dive, p. 68, to discover more.

read and learn

interview

POTTERY AS STORY-TELLING, with DIEGO ROMERO

DIEGO ROMERO IS A THIRD-GENERATION COCHITI PUEBLO ARTIST WHO SPECIALIZES IN POTTERY. HIS POTTERY FORMS ARE BASED ON ANCESTRAL PUEBLO AND MIMBRES CERAMICS WHILE HIS IMAGERY IS INSPIRED BY MODERN COMIC BOOK ART. DIEGO'S PIECES CAN BE FOUND IN MUSEUMS WORLDWIDE.

SIDE VIEW →

Our theme is past and future, so we want to talk to you about how your art combines the old with the new. What are your influences?
As a very young kid, I loved the books *The Iliad* and *The Odyssey*. My dad used to tell me stories from the books at bedtime. Soon after that, I started reading comic books. I've had a fascination with a story that was told through pictures since then.

Coupled with that, is the lack of access to the history of Pueblo Indians. It's available, but I had to do my own research. I was a teenager when I first learned about the Pueblo Revolt and Pueblo history. As an artist, I want to draw from all these fabulous stories.

TOP TO BOTTOM: *The Thinker*, 2008, *Mayans from Mars*, 1996, *Space Madness*, 1996 **RIGHT:** *Prometheus*, 2020

"More than a POTTER, more than an illustrator...what I do is to make a narrative about the human condition."

At 19, I wanted to draw comic books. I started at the Institute of American Indian Arts because it was free for students of American Indian descent. That's where I stumbled upon a pottery class and I instantly had a connection with the instructor, Otellie Loloma.

So you had your heart set on comics from an early age but discovered pottery in college almost by accident... then you combined the two interests.

Pottery became my obsession for a while! Everything became about pottery. I wanted to make pots. I wanted to learn how to dig clay. I wanted to fire them in the traditional way. And much later, I thought to illustrate them.

Did you have a favorite comic book artist?

I did. I do. I mean, there's so many! I'm very immersed in comics, even as an adult. My favorite thing to do is to go to the comic book store. I study new trends and current artists. But I also like the ones that bring back my childhood. Out of those, I would say I love Jack Kirby, who used to illustrate *The Fantastic Four*.

What did you like about his artistic style?

I like the way he depicted outer space. There's actually a word for that—it's called the "Kirby Krackle" [laughs]. It's the way he drew outer space with the planets, quasars, shooting stars... everything so alive and energetic!

Stan Lee was a brilliant comic book writer who focused on the human aspect of the heroes—they loved and lost and went through heartaches—he addressed the human condition, which is something I try to do in my work.

What role did art play in your family?

I come from a family of artists. My father was an art teacher in Oakland and taught junior high school students. From my Indian side of the family, my uncles and aunts were

read and learn

all potters and jewelers and stone carvers. Both of my grandmas were professional artists.

How would you recommend anyone get started?

I tell all my kids when they go off to college, "Take a pottery class at some point." Because once you handle clay, certain people will never leave it. It's so primal and yet so expressive. It's such a connection to our past. I think it might be the oldest art form? Maybe people have been carving ivory since the mastodons (mammoths). But it's right up there. I think it's fair to say mankind has been making ceramic art for 40,000 years.

That is a good ballpark estimate!

It's been around a while and there's a reason; I think humans just really love the tactile quality of taking a a ball of clay and sculpting it into a little pot or figure.

Which step in the process is most satisfying?

I like opening the kiln when it's all done! I also like painting the pot, adding the details. But I also I like building the pots. You know, I don't know if there's a favorite part, but there's definitely a least favorite part of the process... Sanding the pottery, after it's been fired!

Why is that?

I have to wear a mask and go outside. If it's cold, I'm going to be cold. If it's hot, I'm going to be hot. And I'm going to get clay dust in my hair and my eyes and all over my clothes.

How do you begin? Do you have an idea and draw it first?

I usually make a bunch of pots and then the ideas just kind of come to me later. I match the ideas to the pots. Something will inspire me: current events, history, pop art. I might go to a museum, travel somewhere, and see something that inspires me. I might read a comic book, watch the news, or have an amusing anecdote in my own life where I think, "Oh, this would make a funny image." And I try to use humor as a way to get my message

("HERE'S ONE FOR YOU: I am a Chronologist on the absurdity of Human Nature.")

ABOVE: *Space Avanyu,* 2021

automobile?" "Yes." I have a kayak that I'm working on in Southern California that I need to get out and finish up. So this thing about painting on pottery kind of went on to be painting on anything!

You never know where it might take you next. I keep getting new invitations, people asking me, "Come and decorate this in your style." ●

across. People will look at the pot and say, "That's funny," at first take. But then they'll notice, "That's actually a very serious point that he's making."

Does anything else fuel your process, like music?
Yeah, a lot of music that I listened to in high school, like new wave—well back then it was called the *new wave*. Now it's probably oldies [laughs]. Also a lot of reggae. I'm very nostalgic.

Is there anything you haven't tried yet that you've been meaning to?
Oh yeah. I would say I've barely scratched the surface. I'm always looking for something new while going back to things of old. This journey as a potter, ironically, brought me full circle; back to being a printmaker and illustrator—my earlier interests.

People are like, "Well, we love your style. We love your painting on pottery. Could you do it on a skateboard?" "Yes." "Can you do it on an

"Once you handle the clay, certain people will never leave it."

"It's such a connection to our past."

"I think it might be the oldest art form..."

ABOVE: *Able to Leave Tall Buildings*, 2011

read and learn

"Living in harmony with nature is not such a radical idea after all, it has already been possible."

MELATI WIJSEN IS A TWENTY-FOUR YEAR OLD CHANGE-MAKER FROM BALI. AT THE AGE OF TWELVE, MELATI AND HER YOUNGER SISTER ISABEL CO-FOUNDED BYE BYE PLASTIC BAGS, AN ORGANIZATION THAT AIMS TO ELIMINATE SINGLE-USE PLASTICS.

RECENTLY, MELATI BEGAN YOUTHTOPIA, A LEARNING PLATFORM FOR SUPPORTING, TRAINING, AND FUNDING OTHER YOUNG ADVOCATES OF CHANGE. MELATI HOPES TO EMPOWER MILLIONS AROUND THE WORLD TO BE CATALYSTS FOR CHANGE BY GIVING THEM THE TOOLS TO START.

WHAT WAS IT LIKE GROWING UP IN BALI? DO YOU STILL LIVE THERE?
Yes, I still live in Bali. Growing up near the beach was like having nature as our playground. Outside of school and family time, we spent every moment connecting with nature, exploring, and having the wildest adventures.

WHAT WOULD YOU LIKE PEOPLE TO LEARN ABOUT PLASTIC WASTE?
Life before single-use plastic once existed, and we thrived! Living in harmony with nature is not such a radical idea after all, it has already been possible.

IN 2021, YOU WERE FEATURED IN THE DOCUMENTARY *BIGGER THAN US*. WHAT WAS REWARDING AND WHAT WAS CHALLENGING ABOUT THAT EXPERIENCE?
Bigger Than Us was a life-changing opportunity for me. I graduated high school and set off to film this documentary with other young change-makers around the globe. I had to learn interviewing skills on the go; it was really an expanding experience. Suddenly, I was seeing firsthand a lot of big problems

the rest of the world faces and it was difficult to maintain hope. The reward was meeting young people in real life who are making their countries—and the world—a better place.

HOW DO YOU TAKE CARE OF YOUR MENTAL HEALTH WHILE BALANCING ALL OF THIS?

By taking time out and remembering why I am doing all this in the first place. Recently, after an intense three-day festival of learning in Australia, I was able to go whale-watching. I felt how big and beautiful this world is... It renewed my motivation to empower everyone to feel like they can be a part of the solution.

TELL US ABOUT ONE OF YOUR HEROES.

Mohamad Al Jounde is a dear friend of mine. He fled his home in Syria when he was twelve and, instead of sitting in defeat, he built a school for other refugee children in Lebanon.

WHAT'S UP NEXT FOR YOUTHTOPIA?

We just wrapped up our first Learning Man Festival in Australia with Living School—three days of celebrating peer-to-peer learning. Up next, I'm excited about our Mini Grants Program, which will provide financial support for other young change-makers. I'm personally really proud of this because I know firsthand how hard it can be to raise the resources needed to scale your big ideas and solutions. ◼

COLLAGE ART BY KELLETTE ELLIOTT

read and learn

interview with

OUR COVER ARTIST
CHARLOTTE AGER

A LONDON-BASED ARTIST, AUTHOR, AND ILLUSTRATOR CREATING MIXED MEDIA ARTWORK ABOUT NATURE, CULTURE, AND PERSONAL MUSINGS ABOUT LIFE... WHICH OFTEN INCLUDE CAKE AND GRUMPY RABBITS.

I LIKE USING COLOURS THAT CREATE A MOOD

Q: TELL US ABOUT A BOOK FROM CHILDHOOD THAT STILL INFLUENCES YOU TODAY.

A: *Nobody Rides the Unicorn* by Adrian Mitchell, illustrated by Stephen Lambert. It's a beautiful book about a timid young girl who is tricked into betraying a unicorn and capturing them but finds a way to set them free. I always loved it because it had a really soft feeling.

The illustrations aren't bright and happy, but it still made you feel really warm. It still makes me think about how I choose to use colour. I also loved how the main character's quietness and calmness were her strengths. That felt quite unusual in a book and I related to it as a kid who was very shy!

OH I'M NOT SURE ABOUT THIS AT ALL

CHARLOTTE AGER
Zoo

the pound project.

IN THIS BOOK, EACH ANIMAL WAS AN EMOTION, THE RABBIT WAS ANGER

Q: WHAT WOULD BE A DREAM PROJECT?

A: I'd love to illustrate a historical book one day. I like learning about why things have happened and making connections across time. You have to use a lot of imagination to draw these things sometimes because there aren't always photographs. So illustration is an exciting way of bringing moments to life!

THIS FEELS PEA-CEFUL!

I LIKE WHEN DRAWING GETS SILLY, THIS WAS ABOUT A GOAT WHO LEARNS TO MAKE CARROT JAM

Q: WHAT DO YOU DO WHEN YOU ARE IN A DIFFICULT PART OF THE CREATIVE PROCESS?

A: I try and keep playing and realize it's actually good to make lots of mistakes because you learn new things and ways of working. If I'm really stuck I go for a walk in the park and look at trees, people playing, take a big gulp of fresh air! When I get back to my desk I'm usually able to think more clearly.

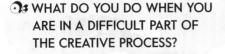

read and learn

interview

Q: ALBUM LISTENED TO RECENTLY?

A: *The Trials of Van Occupanther* by Midlake.

Q: MORNING PERSON OR NIGHT OWL?

A: Morning Mouse.

Q: FAVORITE SNACK WHILE WORKING?

A: Satsumas in winter, strawberries in summer.

Q: ART SUPPLY YOU CAN'T LIVE WITHOUT?

A: The humble 3B pencil.

I USE LOTS OF BLUES!

Q: WHAT'S UP NEXT ON YOUR PLATE?

A: I'm going to be working on a book about plants that make the world better! I love projects where I can learn as well as draw.

MY STUDIO IS VERY MESSY!

read and learn

MAKE, DRAW, WRITE

TYPOGRAPHICAL ART BY YSIDRO PERGAMINO

FOOD OF THE FUTURE

Read the descriptions and future dates, draw what you imagine the food might be:

Nutrients condensed into tiny shapes.

invented in 2053

Are they colorful triangles, cubes, tubes?

Anti-gravity food...does it float? Does it stack impossibly hight?

gravity reduced in 2079

imported in 3017

Food from far-away. Seafood from the ocean floor in Antarctica? Cheeses from the Moon of Saturn?

newly bio-engineered plant life 2088

Don't forget a fancy garnish!

Is there an edible futuristic flower on the side? Drizzle of neon-colored hot sauce?

(did a robot do the cooking?)

WHEN FLOCKS OF DODO BIRDS STILL ROAMED MAURITIUS IN THE 1600s, FRUITS AND SEEDS WERE THEIR SNACKS OF CHOICE...

CHOP FRUIT INTO CHUNKS

ADD TO BOWL AND POUR OVER YOGURT

MIX IT ALL TOGETHER

FOR A FESTIVE LOOK, SPRINKLE CHIA SEEDS OR POPPY SEEDS ACROSS THE TOP BEFORE SERVING

yogurt

MAKE THIS ZINES

and mini-comix

BY: e.haidle

ZINES can be about all sorts of things! With subject matter ranging from day-in-the-life-of style diaries (known as "perzines"), to researched topics (for example, I made a zine all about skunks in 4th grade), or personal opinions about sports, pop culture, music, and books.

The idea of making zines started a long time ago, with sci-fi enthusiasts making "fanzines" in the 1930s. Later, punk rock fans made music zines in the 1970s.

Some people wonder why anyone would spend time making or reading these mini objects? (People who lack imagination.)

Here's what a few of our contributing artists have to say about why they still make, sell, and trade their zines:

Q: Why do you make zines?
A: BECAUSE THEY ARE FUN TO GIVE AWAY!
— Lark Pien

A: THE WORK OF MAKING A ZINE PAYS OFF, RESULTING IN A PIECE OF ART THAT CAN BE CIRCULATED AMONG FRIENDS AND FAMILY. IT'S A GREAT WAY TO WORK OUT IDEAS WHILE ALSO MAKING A FINISHED PRODUCT. — Aaron Bagley

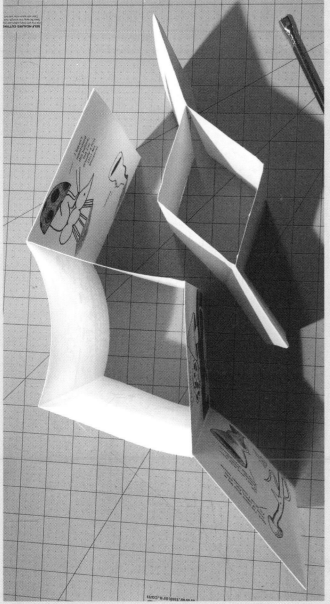

FOLDED ZINE:

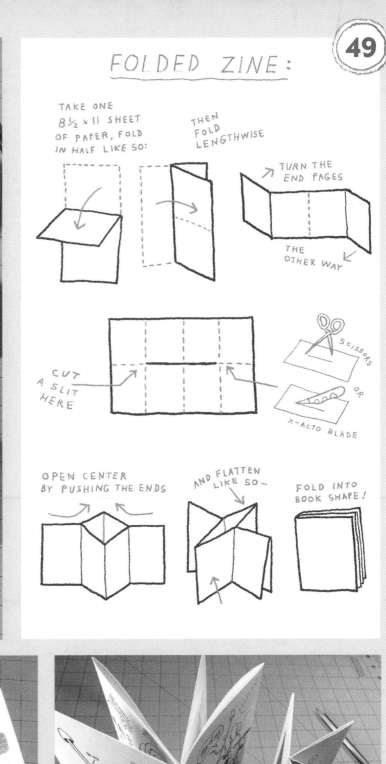

TAKE ONE 8½ x 11 SHEET OF PAPER, FOLD IN HALF LIKE SO:

THEN FOLD LENGTHWISE

TURN THE END PAGES

THE OTHER WAY

CUT A SLIT HERE

SCISSORS

OR

X-ACTO BLADE

OPEN CENTER BY PUSHING THE ENDS

AND FLATTEN LIKE SO—

FOLD INTO BOOK SHAPE!

BOUND ZINE: PLAN YOUR 6-PAGE STORY + COVER DESIGN

back | cover

the plan → | 1 | 2 | 3 | 4 | 5 | 6 |

FRONT ↘ | ↙ BACKSIDE

YOU NEED **TWO** DOUBLE SIDED SHEETS OF PAPER

page 1

| BACK COVER | COVER |
| BACK COVER | COVER |

| 1 | 6 |
| 1 | 6 |

← ✂ CUT

page 2

| 3 | 4 |
| 3 | 4 |

| 5 | 2 |
| 5 | 2 |

← ✂ CUT

FRONT ↘   ↖ FOLD   FOLD ↗   ↙ BACK

2 5
3 4 6
1

CUT, FOLD, STACK, BIND!

COVER

STITCHED ON A SEWING MACHINE ↘

STAPLED ↓

Cat City ™ $2

DENIZENS OF CatCity™ VOLUME ONE

EXISTENTIAL MUSHROOM COMIX

interview:

WITH A ZINE DISTRIBUTOR

Q: HOW DID YOU PICK YOUR NAME?
A: The name relates to our mission: We spread print and physical mediums through digital avenues, employing the future to preserve the past.

Q: WHAT IS ANTIQUATED FUTURE?
A: Antiquated Future is an online store, zine distro, pop-up shop, and tape label that began in 2008 and currently operates out of Portland, Oregon. Over the past fourteen years, we've distributed several thousand different zines, books, tapes, records by independent artists.

Q: WHAT KIND OF DISTRO ARE YOU?
A: We try to carry a really wide range of zines, while still maintaining a curated selection. Personal, historical, music, humor, personal-as-political, literary, how-to, and pop culture are all genres we find ourselves especially drawn to.

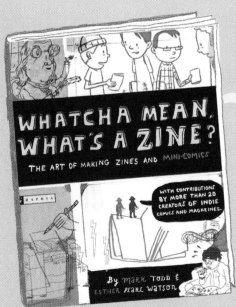

The great thing about zines is the freedom to be able to express your thoughts any way you like. The more raw and honest, the better. It's a world where the weird, absurd, and unique is appreciated.

Ready to try?
We recommend
this ultimate zine guide
by Esther Pearl Watson
and Mark Todd

draw, write, make

DRAWN BY YOU

PROMPT: Draw a prehistoric animal as a pet.

Madeline, age 12,
Auckland, New Zealand

Eliza, age 10,
London, England ↗

I would like to throw a birthday
party with Elasmotherium.
It has a very awesome and big
Party-hat-like horn that would make
my party more fun!!!

Ian Lee, age 8, ↗
Torrance, California, United States

Moritz & Ferdinand, ages 7 & 9, Berlin, Germany ↘

Aadi, age 10, Swizerland

Maria, age 9, Townsville, Queensland, Australia ↘

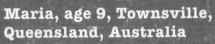

Sam, age 12, Brunswick, Maine, United States

Follow our newsletter to hear about upcoming calls for youth artwork submissions!

A TRANSPORTIVE WORDLESS ADVENTURE
GRAPHIC NOVEL FOR AGES 6 AND UP

Exploring a planet empty of people, a young space traveler happens upon a strange contraption that shows her images of what the planet used to be like. Through this viewfinder, we see Earth as it was compared to Earth as it is: abandoned by people, but still full of amazing things.

With its subtle environmental message and lush, captivating art, this story will leave readers with a renewed sense of wonder for the place we call home.

tundra

HAVE YOU SUBSCRIBED TO ILLUSTORIA YET?

- [ ] i'm doing that next
- [ ] i already did
- [x] need to ask my cat's opinion

check all that apply

WHILE YOU ARE AT IT, GRAB OUR CARRY-ALL TOTE

youth writing

WE ASKED STUDENTS TO WRITE AN IMAGINARY LETTER
TO A PENPAL ABOUT THEIR FUTURISTIC JOB.

MOON GARDEN

from FIGHTING WORDS IN DUBLIN, IRELAND
A MEMBER OF THE INTERNATIONAL ALLIANCE OF YOUTH WRITERS

written by HOLLY KEENA, *age* 16
art by ALEX ALDRICH BARRETT

DEAR KIT,

I HOPE YOU'RE SAFE AND HIGH AND DRY
DOWN ON YOUR GENTLY SPINNING WATER WORLD
I SIT HERE ON ITS LITTLE SISTER MOON
AND WATCH THE FIRES AND HURRICANES UNFURL.

IS IT TRUE THE OCEAN'S MILES ABOVE OLD COASTS?
I DON'T QUITE TRUST THE NEWS BOT THAT DESCRIBED IT.
I'M SORRY THAT OUR LAST TRANSMISSION FAILED,
THE FLOATING MISSILE BONES MUST HAVE MALIGNED IT.

THE FLOWERS IN THE GARDEN BLOOM, BUT DROOP.
TOMATOES, BEANS, AND DILL HAVE ALL GROWN TALL.
I HOPE THE SUGAR CANE STARTS GROWING SOON,
YOUR RECIPES DON'T TASTE THE SAME AT ALL.

THE COLONIES ARRIVE ON SUNDAY NIGHT;
I'LL NO LONGER BE DESPERATELY ALONE.
JUST KNOW THAT EVERY TIME OUR CITY PASSES,
I WAVE AND DREAM OF ONE DAY BEING HOME.

-- YOUR FRIEND

youth writing

WE ASKED STUDENTS TO WRITE AN IMAGINARY LETTER
TO A PENPAL ABOUT THEIR FUTURISTIC JOB.

DEAR JESSE

from 826NYC IN BROOKLYN, NEW YORK CITY, NEW YORK
A MEMBER OF THE INTERNATIONAL ALLIANCE OF YOUTH WRITERS

written by SAMUEL WANG, *age* 16
art by WENG PIXIN

Dear Jesse,

I still can't get over the fact that it's the year 3000! It's like time flies, isn't it? I feel so old living in a new millennium, so many new things to get used to. I don't know about you, but I'm still going to write 2999 on all my papers for the next 4 months. It takes a while to break a habit.

Northern Saturn is finally expanding their frontiers and outposts. I wonder how different this planet will look in 200 years, maybe it'll be completely developed? I love Irohah, literally so glad I moved here. My new boss here is a lot nicer than the one back in Regalair. I have no regrets leaving that place, Mars isn't even that attractive of a planet. My job has become a lot more bearable since switching departments and coming to Irohah. Last Wednesday, we had a staff meeting to eat donuts and discuss strategies to improve the workplace. I suggested we renovate the parking lots to fit more space vehicles. How do all the planets seem to face the same problem of parking??? I wonder if this has always been a problem throughout time...

Anyways, I know you asked me about my job but I had to mention all that earlier. Since I transferred over to the marketing and media department, our work is a lot more fun now. Saturn isn't as developed as Jupiter or Earth, the infrastructure is pretty lacking. The cell service is really spotty, which is regrettable. They're working on developing a full data network across Irohah so it's more compatible with Astrila, but it's been really slow.

I'm excited about a new project I'm designing, which—if successful—would make Irohah a tourist destination. I can't wait to see how things improve! In the architecture department here, they've sketched out future build-out plans.

Enough about what I'm doing! I heard from Tina that you're planning to travel to the Bahamas this summer. Ship me a souvenir please, I've never been to Earth. It's so expensive! I'm so jealous. You'll probably receive this letter really late but the service here is too spotty to text right now.

See you next time, Sam

P.S. Tell your mom I said hi.

draw, write, make

TYPOGRAPHICAL ART BY YSIDRO PERGAMINO

ON OUR PLAYLIST

OUR FAVORITE TRACKS
"I Hear a New World"
"Orbit Around The Moon"

I hear a new world

an outer space music fantasy by JOE MEEK

Joe Meek was an eccentric pioneer of space-age music. With this album, Meek aimed "to create a picture in music of what could be up there in outer space."

To make the other-worldly sounds in this album, Meek recorded the noise of a draining sink, used milk bottles for percussion, and sampled the sounds of a straw blowing bubbles.

As a child, Meek set up an experimental audio station in his parents' garden shed. He later became one of the most influential sound engineers of all time.

LISTEN TO OUR FULL PLAYLIST FOR THIS ISSUE ON SPOTIFY. USE THIS
QR CODE TO DELVE INTO AN HOUR OF EAR-TINGLING TUNES... THE PERFECT
BACKDROP TO JUMP INTO ONE OF THE DIY PROJECTS FROM CHAPTER 3.

NINA COSFORD SKETCHBOOK

Nice, smooth, off-white paper with tasteful rounded corners.

ON OUR DESK

Selected by one of our favorite artists to work with, YUK FUN. YUK FUN was founded by design duo Lucy Cheung and Patrick Gildersleeves in 2014 and is based in Portslade-by-Sea on the south coast of England.

SPEEDBALL BLUE INK

When we're not illustrating, we screen print T-shirts and other stuff! This blue ink is water-based and dries with a nice mottled inky texture.

PENTEL MECHANICAL PENCIL

Drawing with a mechanical pencil makes you feel like a real professional. We like that it's always sharp and you can replace the leads and the eraser on the end.

POSCA PENS

These are really fun to use. Basically painting but with pens!

* FAVORITE SNACK

LUCY

PATRICK

Look and listen

BOOK REVIEW

CONTEST

HARLEY HITCH AND THE MISSING MOON

REVIEW BY: SOFIA C., AGE 8

BOOK BY VASHTI HARDY, ILLUSTRATED BY GEORGE ERMOS

"I like the book because the teachers can be robots. And I also like it because Harley Hitch had a robot dog. I like it because there was a device that made things magically disappear."

REVIEW BY: LUNA B., AGE 6

BOOK BY ASIA CITRO, ILLUSTRATED BY MARION LINDSAY

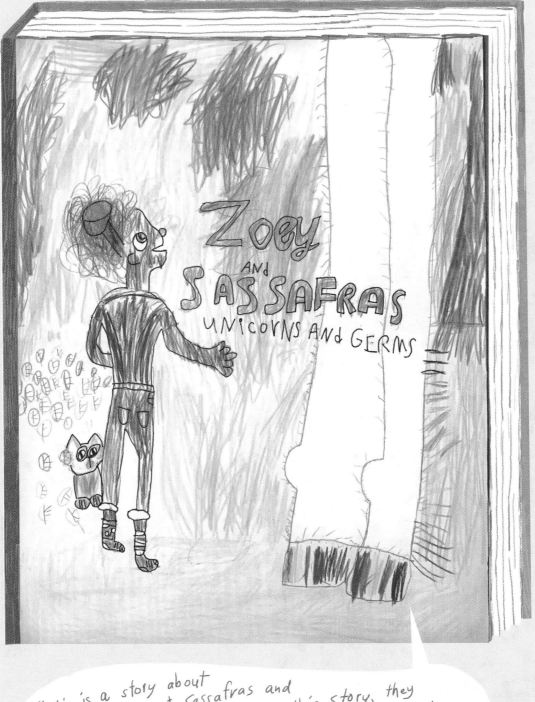

"This is a story about Zooey and her cat Sassafras and they do science together. In this story, they have to take care of a HUMONGOUS baby unicorn who got hurt. Zooey and her mom try to fix the unicorn by testing the germs with different stuff. I like that Zooey goes on many science adventures."

Look and listen

ON OUR BOOKSHELF

Combining art, mythology, and science, this wonder-filled tour of the night sky weaves legends and lore with astonishing scientific facts.

—BY KELSEY OSEID

pair with further reading on COMETS — see page 28

This book reaches back in time to long-ago civilizations, bringing you the most intriguing bits.

—BY CLIVE GIFFORD —ART BY GOSIA HERBA

Finally, a book that answers the question: "Where do rocks come from?"

The answer may be more incredible than you think!

—BY LESLIE BARNARD BOOTH —ART BY MARC MARTIN

← prepare to have some interesting conversations after reading these →

Sometimes the problems of the world seem too big to fix, but starting with something small can yield big results.

—BY
AMANDA GORMAN
—ART BY
CHRISTIAN ROBINSON

Something, someday

Amanda Gorman
#1 New York Times Bestselling Author

Christian Robinson
Caldecott Honor–Winning Illustrator

THE FIRST CAT IN SPACE and the SOUP of DOOM

MAC BARNETT & SHAWN HARRIS

Back again! The second book in this adventure series about unusual space travelers. If you've read book 1, you're no doubt hungry for more...!

—BY
MAC BARNETT
—ART BY
SHAWN HARRIS

Daring to imagine a world beyond the laws of physics and normalcy, these musings from author Alastair Reid—in 1960—find a fresh new life with brilliant illustrations by JooHee Yoon.

—BY
ALASTAIR REID
—ART BY
JOHEE YOON

Supposing...
Alastair Reid · JooHee Yoon

↙ 56 pages of Wondering...

Supposing... you lived next door to a circus lion? ↓ (THEN WHAT?)

Supposing I lived close to a circus and took scraps every day to my favorite lion and learned to speak Lion, and one night the lion escaped and frightened people and I ran up to the lion by myself and spoke to it in Lion until it went to sleep and the manager gave me a free ticket to the circus for the rest of my life...

Look and listen

WANT TO LEARN MORE?

Deeper Dive!

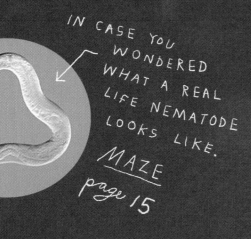

IN CASE YOU WONDERED WHAT A REAL LIFE NEMATODE LOOKS LIKE.

MAZE
page 15

...FROM PAGE 15, MAZE

Check out this article "Ancient Roundworms Allegedly Resurrected From Russian Permafrost" by Meilan Solly in *Smithsonian Magazine* from July 30, 2018 to learn more about ancient nematodes.

...FROM PAGES 24, WE ASKED A POET

We gave our guest poet, Zubair Ahmed, an article called "Is Time Travel Possible?" by Sarah Scoles in *Scientific American* on April 26, 2023.

...FROM PAGE 44, FUTURISTIC FOOD

If you are imagining your futuristic restaurant experience in this writing game, read this article for ideas about 3D printed desserts, robotic dishwashers, and foods served with sounds:

"The Future of Food: What We'll Eat In 2028" by Dr. Stuart Farrimond in *BBC Science Focus* published on May 17, 2019.

* DIAGRAM OF A WORM-HOLE MADE BY A BLACK HOLE
page 24

BLISTERING BARNACLES! HOW DID THAT TRILOBITE GET DOWN HERE?
SEE CREATURE FEATURE,
page 26

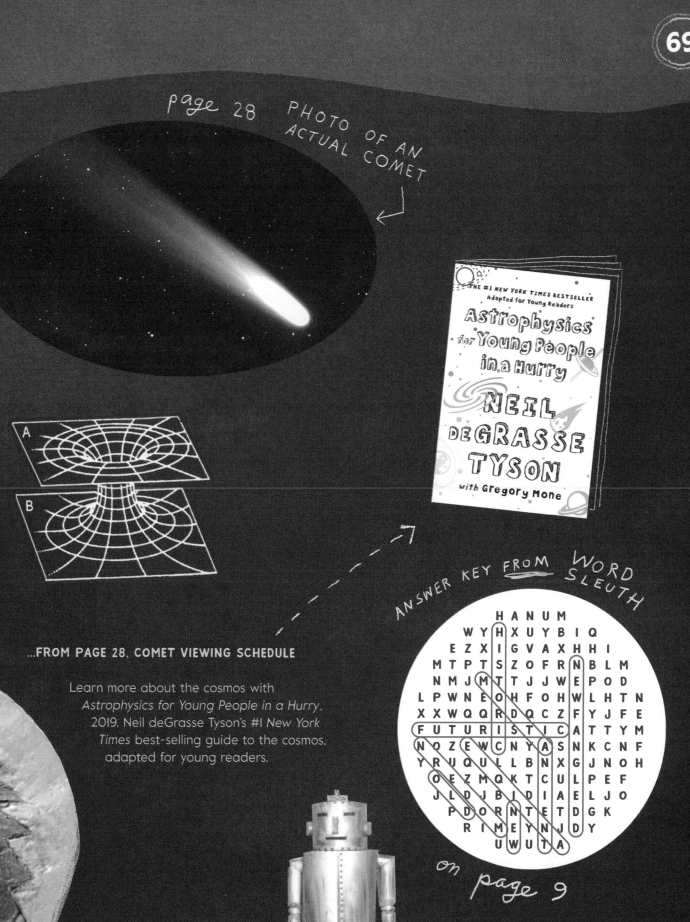

page 28 PHOTO OF AN ACTUAL COMET

Astrophysics for Young People in a Hurry
NEIL deGRASSE TYSON
with Gregory Mone

THE #1 NEW YORK TIMES BESTSELLER
Adapted for Young Readers

ANSWER KEY FROM WORD SLEUTH

...FROM PAGE 28, COMET VIEWING SCHEDULE

Learn more about the cosmos with *Astrophysics for Young People in a Hurry*. 2019. Neil deGrasse Tyson's #1 *New York Times* best-selling guide to the cosmos, adapted for young readers.

on page 9

Look and listen

CHICKEN of the SEA

WRITTEN by VIET THANH NGUYEN and ELLISON NGUYEN

ILLUSTRATED by THI BUI and HIEN BUI-STAFFORD

A band of intrepid chickens leave behind the boredom of farm life, joining the crew of the pirate ship *Pitiless* to seek fortune and glory on the high seas. Led by a grizzled captain into the territory of the Dog Knights, they soon learn what it means to be courageous, merciful, and not seasick *quite* so much of the time.

A whimsical and unexpected adventure tale, *Chicken of the Sea* originated in the then five-year-old mind of Ellison Nguyen, son of Pulitzer Prize-winning novelist Viet Thanh Nguyen; father and son committed the story to the page, then enlisted the artistic talents of Caldecott Honor winner Thi Bui and her thirteen-year-old son, Hien Bui-Stafford, to illustrate it. This unique collaboration between two generations of artists and storytellers invites you aboard for adventure, even if you're chicken. Maybe *especially* if you're chicken.

Back in stock.
Find *Chicken of the Sea* and many others at:
STORE.MCSWEENEYS.NET

Thames
&Hudson

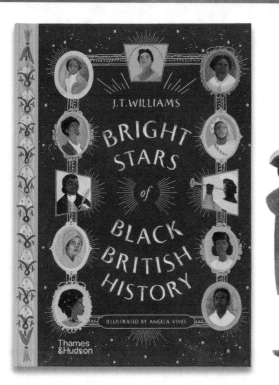

This richly illustrated collection presents the extraordinary life stories of fourteen bright stars from Black British history—from Tudor England to modern Britain—and charts their ongoing influence.

The perfect book for troubled times, this collection of over twenty-five real-life stories shows how heroic acts of kindness can change our world for the better.

"The profiles are well crafted with intriguing, often inspiring details... Bravery, compassion, and initiative go hand in hand in these concise, compelling stories."
—*Kirkus Reviews*

"Inspiring [with] bright, colorful illustrations... Some subjects readers might recognize, while others they may not, making this an especially enlightening read."
—*Booklist*

THE YOUTH WRITING IN THIS ISSUE IS BY STUDENTS FROM

826NYC in Brooklyn, New York City, New York
Fighting Words in Dublin, Ireland

TAKE A TRIP AND VISIT!

FIND A WRITING CENTER NEAR YOU: ➡ YOUTHWRITING.ORG

In every issue of *Illustoria*, students from the The International Alliance of Youth Writing Centers contribute their own writing and art to add a range of voices to these pages. The International Alliance is joined in a common belief that young people need places where they can write and be heard, where they can have their voices polished, published, and amplified. There are nearly seventy centers worldwide. Learn more at www.youthwriting.org.